FIVE

GOLD NUGGETS

D1571770

CHARLES DIXON

Published by Destination Elevation Publishing

ISBN: 978-1737587071

Book Cover Design concept by: Quinton Dixon - Christopher

Book Cover Design by: Frederick Dixon

This book is a collection of memories and experiences of a young boy growing up in a large urban city. This book tells his story of the hilarious events, challenges, and inspirations of life in Harlem, New York.

This book is dedicated to my mother and daughter, Yvonne Dixon and Dionna Dixon

YOU GO! We All GO!

Y5-FOREVER

"People can become as precious as gold. You will go through the fire sometimes, and people may even kick dirt at you; not realizing that you are valuable! But, if you remember your teaching, guidance, and the life lessons you've learned, or even the lessons learned from the collisions of life, you will turn out just fine and will be worth your "weight in gold."

Yvonne

Dionna affectionately and repetitively called this book during the writing process,

"Five Chicken Nuggets."

DD

TABLE OF CONTENTS

Chapter One

STARS COLLIDE

Well before man ever arrived on this Earth, there was gold. The process by which gold is created takes place amongst the stars. Gold is formed when stars explode or collide, only then are the necessary energy and conditions right to create it. Millions of years after the formation of the Earth, someone took a chance and began to dig into the hard crust of the Earth, uncovering the precious metal. One of the oldest recorded civilizations that mined gold was the Inca Empire.

The Incas found gold to be valuable and built their empire upon it. They believed that gold was the sweat of the sun and began mining it. They also used it as a method of trade for goods and services. The ancient Egyptians also found gold to be beautiful and adorned themselves with it. They decorated Pharaohs, statues, and images with this precious metal. Egyptians found that gold had value and wealth, to the point that many wealthy Egyptians had it

1

entombed with them upon death. They believed that they could take the riches of gold with them into the afterlife.

To bring it to the modern day, the history of the United States reveals that gold had value and wealth and was used in exchange for goods and services. The term *gold nugget* was coined and adapted by an old western prospector who found this type of golden rock in the year 1799 A.D. A 17-pound nugget was found in Cabarrus County, North Carolina, the first documented discovery in the United States of America. This discovery sparked the first United States gold rush outside of Red Rock Canyon in Nevada.

In North Carolina, African American *gold rushers*, as they were called helped spur waves of immigration that often led to the permanent settlement of new towns. Activities propelled by gold rushes define significant aspects of the culture in African-American communities. At a time when world money was based on gold, the newly mined gold provided economic stimulus far beyond the goldfields, feeding into the local North Carolina and wider economic booms.

Several of the 49ers were African-American slaves who discovered gold in the 1855 California Gold Rush. The 49er reference pertains to those who took part in the peak gold rush year of *1949*. Nearly three hundred thousand people migrated to California from around the world. These trailblazers, which included many African-American entrepreneurially minded free blacks, both men and women turned California into a destination for those seeking prosperity and opportunity. The phrase, "You're worth your weight in gold," is used to describe someone very valuable.

This metaphoric term dates back to Roman times when slaves were traded for gold based on their weight. The more physically fit and muscular slave a person was, the more value they had. The term "The Gold Standard," referred to gold being the official value of money used as currency. A unit of money, (such as a dollar), is equal to a particular amount of gold. Many believed, and still believe, that if you had gold, you had wealth and value and people were willing to do about anything to get their hands on it.

Men and women still search for gold. And today, gold can be found in the most unexpected places; it just might be right under your nose. People become gold when life explodes in front of them, challenging them to become better people and citizens. Under extreme heat and pressure, gold nuggets are sometimes broken down into dust for one reason or another. Broken down or not, gold still has value.

Someone once said that *nothing good will ever come out of Harlem, New York*. Well, I beg to differ. Gold was in Harlem, waiting to be discovered.

Chapter Two

HARLEM

I was a young boy, full of wonder and curiosity, growing up. I grew up in Harlem between 110th Street Central Park West, and West 155th Street. Interestingly enough, many, many years ago this area was inhabited by a Native American band, The Wecquaesgeek, and dubbed the "Manhattoe" by Dutch settlers. In 1658, a Dutch governor established a settlement named "Nieuw Haarlem," named after "Haarlem," in the Netherlands. Dutch and European settlers settled in the area, which was mostly farmland and undeveloped territory until the early 1900s. As New York's population grew, residential and commercial expansion moved northward, and the development of Harlem was inevitable. This was the beginning of a large-scale building program in New York City.

Art Deco architecture had found its way into the Harlem building program and beautiful buildings began to rise from the dirt to include the famous brownstone designs. In the early 1900s, fueled by migration from the West Indies and Southern United States to escape racial persecution, Harlem became predominantly black and sparked *The Harlem Renaissance*. The Harlem Renaissance became a symbol of the African-American struggle for civil and economic equality while emerging as a flourishing center of black culture. It was a wonderful time of an intellectual, spiritual, and cultural revival of African-American music, dance, art, fashion, literature, theater, politics, and scholarship.

Centered in this notable place and time in American history forever altered the encounters of black and white New Yorkers and had far-reaching effects on American society as a whole. Famous historical sites that reside in Harlem include 125th Street, Apollo Theater, Cotton Club, the United House of Prayer For All People, 116th Masjid Malcolm Shabazz Muslim Temple, Central Park, The Hotel Theresa, and Spanish Harlem. The Hudson River borders Harlem on the West and the East River borders Harlem on the East. Harlem residents prided themselves on looking well-groomed and professional.

Black Americans symbolized by their rich and diverse culture established the Black Church, The Universal Negro Improvement Association, and The National Association For The Advancement of Colored People (NAACP). These organizations worked diligently in Harlem to foster better living conditions and opportunities for "Harlemites." During this time, men and boys wore hats and suit coats with clean shoes. Women proudly displayed wonderful hair do's and colorful dresses. Everyone greeted each other with hello, peace, or grace as they passed you in the street or at the store. Children treated adults with the utmost respect and the adults were part of the community that shared in the raising and teaching of good values to all the children.

Seventh Avenue and 125th Street were called the "Great Black Way." The neighborhood contained the Salem Methodist Church, The studio of James Van Der Zee, Harlem's most famous photographer, The African Memorial National Book store, The Mafia Diamond Jewelry store, The M. Smith Photo Studio, Blumstein's Department store, Frank's restaurant, Oscar Hammerstein's Play House, Harlem Opera House, and The Savoy.

Many "Harlemite" historians shared many events of the Harlem of the past. One was an old man who owned a small candy shop across the street from our building. The candy shop had survived many generations and kids still lined up to buy candy during the day. It always took about thirty minutes to buy one pack of candy or a soda because it came with a story. He would often begin with, *"I have a story to tell you, kids,"* and would tell you about the great Harlem Renaissance and how people dressed so elegantly and spoke so politely and eloquently. He would talk about the great depression how the community stuck together to survive or when the Apollo Theater was built and how he met Dr. Martin Luther King, Jr. and Malcolm X.

He pointed to several buildings in the neighborhood and told us how some of the best Art Deco immigrant sculptures had designed and chiseled the artwork right into the building's stone. He also shared stories with us about how the community and

6

people had changed. He told us stories about buffalo soldiers of the past and the Tuskegee Airmen who fought in World War II, and how our African American brothers served this great country so that we can have an opportunity to get a good education and be free to live our lives. I listened with the other kids as we all stood there thinking, *we just wanted our candy.*

The local barber was also a historian, he knew everybody and everything about everything. Politics, money, entertainment, and people, you name it. When you went to the barbershop, you could find out about who was running for mayor, governor, senator, or president. The local barbershop was a community meeting place where everyone was welcome to voice their opinion and debate about any topic under the sun. Harlem also had some of the best soul food restaurants in New York City that provided fine dining, live music, and dancing. Top chefs and all-around great cooks from all over the world migrated and bought recipes and diverse culinary cuisine to the neighborhood church kitchens and storefront establishments.

Chapter Three

MONDAY

It was the mid-1960s and a warm spring morning, the sun was still rising in the sky and there was a calm breeze blowing. The type of breeze that would move the brown and orange curtains in my bedroom just a little to let you know it was there. There was a loud noise from the garbage truck and men loading and dumping the metal trash cans onto the truck.

It was your 6:00 a.m. alarm clock, stating that it was Monday morning and time to get ready for school. The impact of the noise was amplified when you have a practical joker sibling that opens your bedroom window. The loud noise jolted you out of the bed, Crash! Bang! Floor. That is where you ended up, on some mornings.

More noisy sounds came in through the window by the street sweeper and some guy screaming "Butterman;" "Egg Man." It was a typical morning in New York, New York, King of the Hill, A #1. Mom had already knocked on the bedroom door frame with my first warning to get up. I had already gotten back in bed and was looking at the ceiling and daydreaming about my weekend activities.

I remember how it all started on Friday afternoon when me and my brothers walked to 125th Street to watch men set up a stage and decorate for the annual Harlem Day celebration. This was a one-day event of encouragement and fellowship in Harlem for New Yorkers and beyond. And to showcase the community's rich economic, political, and cultural history. During this event, all the stores on 125th Street decorated their storefronts, and the Apollo Theater opened its doors and provided entertainment on the stage.

Many well-known African American leaders were keynote speakers at the event and many famous R&B artists would stop in and excite the crowd with their music and poetry. One of my most memorable performances was the "Alvin Ailey Dance Company." They wore beautiful floral and authentic African costumes and were a group of young African-American dancers who forever changed the perception of American dance. The event became so popular that it was extended to an entire week and is now known as "Harlem Week."

Friday evening, I visited Spanish Harlem, at the Annual Puerto Rican Spring Festival. There were carnival rides and cart vendors that handed out shaved ice in flavors like coconut, Pina Colada, and pineapple. One vendor had decorative peeled oranges and another, Cuchi-Fritos. Off in the distance, you could hear the sound of a trumpet, conga, and guitar. The Latin soul music would draw you closer and you would see couples dancing the salsa and people clapping with the music and singing. Neighbors, friends, and families were all enjoying themselves while celebrating the culture of the community and Harlem.

Also, I remembered, that on Saturday morning, I went to the West End Theater on W 125th Street. It was a triple feature karate movie with Bruce Lee, all for seventy-five cents. It took me an entire week of extra chores to raise the one dollar I needed for the movie. The extra twenty-five cents went towards snacks. I then went to the community center down the street and played softball until the evening.

I remembered going to church services on Sunday, the church provided guidance and value to the community. If you paid attention, you would hear a great message from some of the greatest men to ever preach in Harlem. Followed up by inspirational soul-moving musicians who played gospel hymns with trombones, saxophones, tubas, trumpets, and drums. For most services, I fell asleep and was often poked by my mom or brothers to wake up before my Dad saw me. Dad didn't like us falling asleep at church services and the penalty hurt.

I couldn't remember most of the services per se. I remember Sunday school because if you were good, the teacher would give you a lollipop after the class. Dad taught us cherished life lessons from his past, and one lesson he taught us was that we should give God thanks every day for all He has done, so I thanked God for the lollipop.

I am up now, stretching, yarn, and looking around thinking, It's still Monday and why? It's the first day of the week and always hard to get up and get moving. The weekend went by in a flash, and it seemed like it was all a big dream. I didn't do any of my chores over the weekend and this room is a mess; Mom is not going to be happy with me. I then rustle up Y4. We shared a room and looked out for each other. "Let's go, Bro, before Mom comes back."

It's like a military school at home, thanks to soldier Dad. We line up for everything, showers, meals, chores, grooming, hugs, and allowances. Go. Go. Go! Wash, dress, eat, and get to school. It is my turn now to get in the bathroom… OMG! OMG…Y2 did a #2. Why me, Lord? I have learned how to hold my breath pretty well at the community center during swimming practices. The bathroom had a small window that let in fresh air. I looked like a puffer fish with my face stuck to the window as I inhaled fresh air. Bang! Bang! Bang! On the door. Come on out, I got to go man! That is Y4 and my partner in crime.

Now, it's time for breakfast, I am dressed in my blue jeans, knock-off Pro Ked's that still had the blue and red stripe, and my favorite striped polo shirt. I have always dreamed of becoming an astronaut when I grow up. At the breakfast table, I sink into a daydream about walking on Mars with Robbie the Robot from the *Lost in Space* television show. My space suit is orange, and my helmet is white with an oxygen hose running from my backpack. I am using my NASA shovel to dig into the crust of the planet for scientific samples to send back to Earth.

Wait! I saw something moving in the distance towards me and the Robot said "Danger" "Danger" and then. Y1 quickly snapped me back to reality with a slap to the head, saying come on boy, hurry up and eat. You are gonna be late. He ruined a perfectly good daydream. Now! Y1 thought he was *God's gift of big brothers*. If there was a big brother election, even though I was too young to vote; I demand a recount!

Chapter Four

THE GREAT MIGRATION

D ad and his family moved to New York City in the early 1930s. His father: my grandfather moved the entire family to the north by train to escape the racial persecution in the South. Two parents and twelve children arrived in Harlem, in the early 1930s. Dad told us that he and his family weren't allowed to eat in the train car or use the bathrooms. Black people had to use the cars that carried mail or livestock to eat or use the toilet.

My family was not by themselves during this period in American history. Over six million African Americans took part in the "Great Northward Migration" or the "Black Migration" to escape racial persecution and hopes of better living conditions and economic stability. They traveled by horse and buggy, train, and boat and some even walked or hitch-hiked to escape the poor conditions in the south. These were very difficult times for those migrating and they faced many challenges. Radical whites put up roadblocks to

13

deter black people from crossing through their towns. Black people were beaten and hung from tree limbs if they were caught in a white man's yard or property. Some white people supported and helped black people migrate from the South. However, some businessmen and politicians saw it as an opportunity to get rich and imposed migration fees on blacks.

Dad once told us a story about a group of white men with torches that showed up on the family property in South Carolina early one morning. He said they were screaming profanity and racial slurs and threatening to burn the houses down if the *"niggers"* did not come out! But, as Dad said, they had no idea how large the family was or how many small family homes in the back woods surrounded them. My dad's uncles, brothers, and sisters were avid hunters and knew the swamp area behind the homes by night and horseback. A family friend who was a white man stepped out of the woods along with my granddad, great uncles, cousins, and friends. When the Ku Klux Klan saw the group of people coming out of the woods with shotguns, they turned and rode away. Grandpa and his brothers built a stone barrier with river rock and mud to deter intruders from coming onto the family property.

Dad told me that it was very tough back in those days. Some people even starved to death and became very ill due to the lack of food and medicine. Many people didn't have much and dreamt of finding gold and striking it rich. People could be found at the water's edge of the Congaree River in South Carolina just about every day panning for gold. They believed in an old treasure tale passed down from generation to generation about a Confederate supply boat that was said to have overturned with thousands of gold coins and ingots in the river. Most days, no one found a spec of gold dust.

However, despite their circumstances during the migration, they treated each other with respect, kindness, and consideration. Thankful, and sharing what they did have as a family. People would say to each other; "You're as good as gold." My dad said that if it wasn't for family and friends caring and sharing what they had, they wouldn't have survived.

Chapter Five

FIVE GOLD NUGGETS

Seven of us were in a large apartment on the 4th floor, this was my parents, four boys, and one girl, the princess. Mom thought it was fun to give us all numbers. We are now known as "Y5." I'm lucky Y3, Yes! The middle child, or, as I like to say, the brains of the operation.

As you entered the apartment there was a long white hallway. It was one of my chores to clean the fingers and handprints off the walls and door. Mom would say, *"The dirty handprints didn't get there by themselves."* The kitchen was the first room to the right as you entered the apartment. It was a large room painted canary yellow with a matching yellow colored stove and a white refrigerator. There was a white double wash sink along the right-side wall and a long shelf along the left wall. Under the shelf hung an assortment of pots and pans. Oh yes, I remember there were yellow cabinets over the shelf. There was also a small rectangular table in the corner.

This is where we pick up our lunch or snacks for school daily or do our homework.

Halfway through the kitchen off to the left was another small room that was painted white with red borders, and it had a tub washer and an ironing board. Dad attached a clothes-hanging contraption to the ceiling with hooks and rope that lowered, so it could be reached. We would hang our clothes on it to dry. Dad, (Mufasa the King), as we kids called him, was a tall, medium build strong brown-skinned man. My dad was raised in the South, served in the United States Army, was a disciplinarian, and plumber, and was a preacher with a strong faith in God, family, and community service.

Mom was a short slender woman also from the South. Her skin was like a cup of cocoa and soft like butter. She could often be heard singing throughout the apartment. She was a teacher, referee, cook, and drill sergeant. She was very sweet with a kick of spicy sauce and supported her family and community. Brother Y1 was the eldest, short like Mom, and was Dad and Mom's pride and joy, a practical joker, the Y5 chain gang leader, and a good brother.

Brother Y2, the Gentle Giant, was the tallest brother like Dad. He was very caring and protected his younger siblings.

Brother Y3, that is me. I was a preemie baby, a little guy, short and slim. Also mischievous, street-smart, and mouthy on the surface. Grandma's sweet, precious "Charlie Brown" underneath.

Brother Y4, was my best bud, "The baby boy" Mommy's boy. He was short heavy set, and ate all the time, smart as a whip.

Sister Y5, "The Princess." One day, Mom assembled us all in the living room and announced that she was having a girl! I believe my response was *"Who needs a girl and why?"* Followed by no girls allowed on the chain gang, from Y1 and Y2. Mom allowed us to vent and then stated that the apartment was going to be reorganized, so the Princess would have her own room. "What!" Y1 replied, he was in line to get his own room and had his eyes on that area. *"Not going to happen,"* replied the gang as we laughed and said, *"Back to cell block #6 buddy."*

It was a warm summer afternoon in Harlem and my mother called Y1 and told him to go get our dad and hurry. We practiced this exercise many times with Mom and Dad to prepare for this day. We all had our jobs to do. My job was to get Mom's slippers, and overnight bag, and hold the apartment door open for her. Dad and Y1 arrived shortly and left for the hospital. Later that day, the phone rang, and I heard Grandma say, *"It is a girl; it is a girl!"*

Grandma had been staying with us for over a week to help Mom out. Baby girl was small, cute, and bossy, and she was totally protected by four soldier brothers. She could do no wrong and had us eating out of her hands. She was a "total tattler," who would put your business on the breakfast or dinner table in a heartbeat. Y2 oversaw the princess's security detail, she could not be touched by anyone, and he was the princess's favorite. You can't pick your family; all you can do is learn how to live with them. Or try to return them on Monday like a package.

Chapter Six

THE UN

We lived in a large tan brick apartment building off 7th Avenue in the hundred teens block. There were five floors with two apartments on each floor. No elevator was in the building and there were 19 steps on each staircase with tan marble and brown rod iron decorative stairs leading to each level. The walls were painted beige and had a decorative swirling pattern on the walls. At each stairwell landing there was a large, green-painted window that only opened a few inches to allow fresh air in.

Families from all over the world lived in the building, which made our community remarkably diverse. On the 5th floor, lived a Canadian family and an African family. On the 4th floor, lived an African American family and a Jewish family. On the 3rd floor, lived a Hawaiian family and an English family. On the 2nd floor, lived a Caucasian family and a Caribbean family. And on the 1st floor lived a Caucasian family. We all got along fine.

One day after taking a school field trip to the Lower East Side of Manhattan where the United Nations building is located. My friends and I got the bright idea to rename our building the United Nations. We gathered all the chalk we could, the big round kind, and wrote in Big Bold Letters on the front of the building (UNITED NATIONS). Well, the building superintendent who was responsible for the care and upkeep of the building did not appreciate the literature on the property, so he washed it off!

Now, we had learned from our field trip to the UN that sometimes you have to fight for democracy. We gathered in our clubhouse, which was a large old box, and voted to take additional peaceful action. We wrote it again, and he washed it off. We wrote it again, and he washed it off. We then called an emergency UN meeting and voted to make it bigger with blue chalk. He washed it off with a warning to our parents to tell us to stop. We regrouped in a small corner of the building to discuss the situation. We had representatives from every nation in the building and came up with a plan to support our democracy. We found a small spot behind a column at the entrance of the building and scratched the letters "UN" into the concrete with an old nail we found. And until this day, we still refer to the building on 7th Avenue as the UN.

Chapter Seven

SNOOPY

Not only millions of immigrants migrated to New York City, but they also brought all types of exotic animals with them. Everyone had at least one pet in the UN. The Canadian family on the 5th floor had cats and the African family had a large talking Cockatoo. On the 4th floor, the Jewish family had a Poodle and on the 3rd floor the Hawaiian family had a large German Shepherd named "Major." The English family had several small yellow Canary birds. On the 2nd floor, the Caucasian family had two small Yorkshire Terriers. One man in the neighborhood had a small monkey that sat on his shoulder and there was talk of another man that had a tiger that lived on 116th street. I never saw a tiger, but if I was to have a pet, then my choice would be a tiger.

Grandma showed up one day and said I have a surprise for my little "Charlie Brown." Grandma was in love with the whole Peanuts Charlie Brown cartoon and decided that this would be her grandson's nickname. I despised this name because of the sibling teasing all the time. Charlie Brown. Charlie Brown. Charlie Brown, "You're a Blockhead, Charlie Brown." UGH! Grandma reaches into a basket and pulls out a small dog. She said it was a Beagle and his name is Snoopy. I'm thinking, you have got to be kidding me, Grandma! She said now you have a dog "Charlie Brown and Snoopy," it's so cute. I have never liked pets, especially dogs. I was traumatized by Mr. Hawaiian's dog "Major."

Now Major was the biggest dog I've ever seen in person. He was brown and tan with large teeth and a big head and feet that seemed as big as mine. He had a thick linked chain around his neck that dragged and clanked when he ran. I could ride this dog like a pony, but only in my dreams. You could hear his bark throughout the apartment building and this dog was mean. Mr. Hawaii would explain to my parents all the time that he was just a pup and would never eat your kids. "Whaaaat! The!.. Eat your kids?" My imagination went wild. I only weighed 45 pounds and would only be an appetizer for Major. I would sacrifice Y2 he was bigger and would provide a better meal and an escape route for me and Y4. I'm just kidding; relax. Y1 definitely would be sacrificed for the survival of the pack. Mr. Hawaii got a kick out of this "accidental Major release act," twice a week. When Major would chase me down the steps, Woof, Woof, Woof, growling and barking, to a young boy; It sounded like "I'm gonna eat you!"

Grandma asked me if I liked the dog, and I answered no ma'am! She said why not? I said, *"Grandma, I just don't like dogs."* The princess spoke up and Y4 said can we have him? You could see in

Grandma's eyes that she wanted me to have the little dog to complete her Charlie Brown and Snoopy thing. She told the princess and Y4, yes, and with excitement they grabbed Snoopy up and took him to her room. The dog barked all night long and I had to put a pillow over my ears to get some sleep. The next morning, I woke up, and to my surprise, the snoopy dog was lying on my shirt on the floor next to my bed sleep. That's just great, I called out to the princess to come and get her dog out of my room. Mom replied and said Y3, take that dog outside so he can do his business. I replied politely, Mom, it's not, she interrupted me and said did you hear what I said, "Yes Ma'am, (Rack N, Frak N), stupid dog." "What did you say?" "Nothing ma'am."

I got dressed, grabbed the leash, and walked downstairs with Snoopy. It took forever to get downstairs because Snoopy had little feet and could only take a half step at a time. I was not picking him up and just pouted and waited until he got down the steps. I'm now outside with this stupid dog standing in the stupid rain. He does his business and I'm the one who has to pick up the stupid poop and dispose of it, *stupid dog!* I thought to myself, if he somehow got off his leash and ran away, I would be free from this dog. I unhooked the leash from his collar and ran away as fast as I could. This dog thinks we are having fun and runs after me just as fast. I then go into the grocery store and close the door behind me.

The grocery man knew me and said good morning. What are you doing up so early? I told him I was running away from a dog outside, he walked to the door and there was Snoopy just sitting there wagging his tail. The man said, *"Oh, that's Snoopy your new dog."*

"What?!" "Yes, your grandma stopped by yesterday and showed him to me." "Charlie Brown and Snoopy," that's very cute. Does everyone in the neighborhood know about this dog? I put the leash back on Snoopy's collar and head back upstairs.

For many days, weeks, and months after that moment, Snoopy stuck to me like glue. Mom said he would bark and look sad when I was at school and immediately perk up when I got home. He growled at Y1, which gave me a warm feeling for the dog inside and I was bonding with Snoopy and teaching him tricks with an old tennis ball.

One day returning home from a walk, Snoopy began to let out a low growl as we approached the building. Once I got closer, I could see that Mr. Hawaii was on the front steps with Major who was lying across the step blocking anyone from crossing. Major stood up and began to bark at us when all of a sudden Snoopy began to bark in a loud-pitched tone that showed dominance over Major and he stopped barking backed up and sat down next to Mr. Hawaii. My mouth was wide open as Mr. Snoopy Dog led us both into the building and up to the apartment. He got a tummy rub for that one, good dog!

Chapter Eight

HALLOWEEN

Our Harlemite family was a bunch of practical jokers. Dad had this silver-looking shock book that he purchased from the joke store on 42nd Street in downtown Manhattan. He would invite you to open the book to read a passage and when you did, the book would give you a shock. Many people cursed him out over that book. Mom had several pairs of vampire's teeth and when you least expected it she would lunge out at you trying to bite you and say, *"Come here my little piggy,"* and let me bite you. I did not like to be scared and always tried to stay ahead of the practical jokes by spoiling the joke before it started. I would tell Mom that I could see the fake teeth in her mouth before she could chase us, and I would open Dad's shock book with gloves on. The gang always said that I was a "sour puss" and no fun.

Halloween gave us a fun-filled outlet for games and practical jokes. The entire UN would dress up and share meals. There was also a competition for the family who had the scariest costume or comical dance routine on the main floor of the building. The Canadian family had won several years in a row. I think they were actors because they were good every year and performed like they were in a television show. Last year they had music, lights, and tap danced in their clown costumes. This year, the Caribbean family was planning something big and painted their apartment door bright red and put a small table with taffy candy in a bowl out front for the kids. We would stop every day and grab a piece of candy heading up or down stairs from our apartment. Their apartment door was always slightly open, and we would try to peek in to see what they were up to.

You could smell a wonderful aroma coming from the apartment and then Mr. Caribbean would say, *"What are you boys doing? I can see you by my door."* We would run away. Y5 always wondered about Mr. and Mrs. Caribbean because they were super nice and always offered you candy and specifically mentioned to me that it would fatten me up. This thought always worried me, I read the story of Hansel and Gretel, they were lured into a home made out of candy and almost became a witch's dinner. I was determined not to wind up on someone's table with an apple in my mouth, so I always kept my distance.

Halloween night is here and of course, I'm dressed like Charlie Brown. Ugh! My grandma bought me a yellow and black shirt like the Peanuts Charlie Brown character and made me wear it and walk with Snoopy. The entire UN was buzzing with music and fun, everyone's apartment door was open and children from the neighborhood filled their bags with candy as they moved from floor to floor. As you passed by the Caribbean's apartment you noticed Ms. Caribbean standing in the dark hallway smoking a cigarette and her eyes seemed to be glowing and then a voice heavy with a Caribbean accent asked. *"Do you children want some candy?"* We saw Ms. Caribbean, who was a tall slender lady with long grey and black braids coming down her back and shoulders, and an image of a black robe or coat that seemed to float as they moved toward us. She repeated *"Do you kids want some candy?"* it will make you happy.

The Caribbeans had scared the "Bejesus" out of us, and we ran down the stairs screaming. (Nope)! Mom and Dad were in on the gag, they were good friends with the Caribbean family and would visit them often. Dad built a wooden platform with wheels that would seem to make them float. The Caribbean family won the prize for the scariest costumes. Mom and Dad knew that we did not want to stay with Ms. Caribbean and would use the witch card on us if we weren't ready for church service on time.

Mom would say if you are not ready for church on time, I will drop you off at the witch's apartment until I get home. "Nope..El No!" We were running down the apartment hallway hoping to try to get our shoes on and downstairs we went to Church. Other times, Mom would say with a smile looking at me and Y4, that Ms. Caribbean was a nice lady and was lonely because her children were older and had moved away. She has offered to babysit your kids if we needed some help. I'm thinking, *"You didn't sell us on that one Mom!"* We never stayed at that lady's apartment. Not me! Nope!

Chapter Nine

PUBLIC SCHOOL
NEW YORK CITY

Once out of the building and to freedom. We immediately met up with school buddies going the same way. The usual elementary school gossip would start with someone saying. Did you see the Batman show yesterday? Or Superman? Did the brown-skinned girl with the pink bow in her hair talk to you yesterday? Are you gonna talk to her in English class? These were conversations on the way to school. PSNY was a large tan and blue brick building a few city blocks from my home. It took about 15 minutes to casually walk with schoolmates to and from school. On a running late day, you could cut through the "Forbidden Alley."

At school, it's back in line with your class. All my brothers and my sister went to the same public elementary school in Harlem. Y1 was responsible for the chain gang and fussed at me as we walked to and from the big house. *"Hey, Y3 don't pet that dog, walk faster, and tie your shoe. I'm telling Dad about you when we get back home."* By the time I got to school, I needed an ice-cold carton of milk to calm my nerves.

Once I broke away from Y1, I took a shortcut to the lunchroom kitchen to find my aunt who worked there. Ms. B, as we kids called her, would always slide me a cold carton of milk before classes started. *"Mmm, that's some good milk."* She always told me that she understood me because she explained that she too is a middle child. She would tell me to drink my milk, get a good education, grow up, and move the hell out of the house because the middle child is a life sentence.

Time for classes, the bell is ringing followed by the principal's address, pledge of allegiance to the United States of America flag, and prayer. Yes, prayer was in public schools, and we turned out simply fine. This was followed by my classes, in social studies, science, mathematics, and gym. Then followed by lunch and English class. School classes hurt my head and I didn't appreciate all the homework. Every class sent a homework assignment home that was due the next day. I was thinking, why should I go to school because I'm doing just as much studying at home? Maybe if I ran away with the Ringling Bros Barnum & Bailey Circus, I could escape all the homework.

Have you ever done something that your parents told you not to do? Oh well, I am not by myself. Mom told us many times, *"Never go down that alley!* *"You boys hear me?"* *"Yes, Mother Dear!"* I was thinking, why? The alley is a shortcut to school and the big boys run through the alley every day.

I'm a big boy, right Y4? Yup. Dad said we are big boys now. That is all I needed to hear. It's about 2:45 p.m. on a cloudy afternoon, classes are over and me and Y4 are waiting for Y1 & Y2 to come and walk us home. They are at basketball team practice. It's not like they were getting the ball in the hoop. Airball after airball, these kids were bad basketball players. Y4 said, *"I'm bored and hungry, let's go home." "We must wait for Y1." "We are gonna be here all day and I need to go to the bathroom."* I've noticed that whenever Y4 didn't want to do something he would play the bathroom card and it worked every time. I said, *"Let's go ask Y2."*

I knew that Y2 couldn't hear my request through the fence and the noise of the boys' basketball game. The gesture is what counted in my mind. I raised my voice and yelled, *"Through a hole in the fence. Hey! Y2, we are going home."* As expected, there was no response.

Oh well, I did my part, *"Let's go Y4."* My home was exactly four city blocks from our school, and you could see the building from the main avenue. While walking to the avenue from school about halfway down the street was the "Forbidden Alley."

It is set between two large buildings with steep steps at both ends and a ramp. Trash cans lined the alley and clotheslines with drying clothes swung overhead that blocked the sun and made the alley look even scarier. We stood there looking at it, contemplating if we ran, could we make it? Mom's voice comes to my mind, but I shake it off. The alley will save us time and I can get Y4 home quicker. I think, what would Batman do? I take a deep breath and look at Y4, he is all in as Robin would be. I yell, *"Run!"* We broke down the ramp full speed dodging trash and a cat. Little legs don't fail me now! Running, running, we almost made it to the ramp on the other side of the alley. When somebody grabbed us from behind and pushed us to the ground.

My heart stopped! I heard Y4 yell, *"Stop pushing me!"* I tried to turn around, but someone pushed me to the ground. Then a voice said, *"I'm telling Dad about both of you."* Breathe, it was only Y1, still in his basketball shorts and tee shirt. Breathing heavily and unable to talk yet, I could see Y2 coming down the alley. They slapped us on the head and read us our constitutional rights as they escorted us back to the schoolyard and demanded that we better not move, and we didn't. Once I could breathe and get myself together, I saw Y2 take Y4 with him into the gym bathroom.

I began to think about what had happened, my plan was thorough, and I had covered all the bases; so, I thought, someone talked. I stood up Looking around and there he was, the snitch! (Butter Bean) smiling at me and saying you're in trouble, you're gonna get a wuppen while patting his backside. I just looked at him with my Batman look and said in my mind, *"I'm going to get you bean boy!"*

Butter Bean was a classmate, a chubby boy, whom, I had fought in the past. I had skills, like a little Muhammad Ali, float like a little butterfly, and sting like a little bee.

We fought one day after school and well after I hit Butter Bean twice, he hit me, and I could hear the announcer in my head say, "Down goes Frazier," and "Down goes Frazier again." Joe Frazier was my dad's favorite heavyweight boxer. Before I could shake it off, he grabbed me and sat on me. "Say, uncle boy. Say, uncle!" "UNCLE!" I thought he was gonna crush me, so I gave up. We were not friends, and I was confident due to his actions that he told Y1 that I went in the alley. I watched as Y2 came back with Y4 who was crying. "What's wrong man?" Y2 said, "Dad's gonna kill you!"

Tomorrow's gonna be a long day at PSNY. The entire basketball team and the coach saw what happened in the alley.

Chapter: Ten

THE BROWN SKIN GIRL

On many days playing in the neighborhood, girls and boys would play together. The girls seemed to outnumber the boys three to one and it wasn't uncommon to see a boy turning a rope so the girls could jump. The bigger boys would even turn two ropes for the girls so they could jump Double Dutch. Double Dutch is a game in which two long jump ropes turning in opposite directions are jumped by one or more jumping simultaneously. These Harlemite girls were very good and even had a Coach with uniforms. One afternoon coming from the park with Snoopy, I stopped at the playground and watched a Double Dutch competition. Snoopy was a girl magnet and they all wanted to pet and rub him. He would lie on his side so the girls could rub his tummy. I'm thinking "What a HAM."

Some girls would talk to me, saying hello and what's your name? I responded politely but was not interested in a specific girl until I saw the brown-skinned girl jumping rope. She went to my school and was in one of my classes. I only saw her in passing and was too shy to say anything to her. I stood up and looked her way even though the other girls were talking to me, everything faded in the background as we both made eye contact. Snoopy yanked the leach to pull me out of my daze, he had an expression on his face that seemed to say, *Come on man snap out of it.*

She wore a pink ribbon in her hair. She is beautiful, with light brown skin, long black hair, green eyes, and a pretty blue dress. She sits two chairs in front of me and occasionally looks back in my direction. Behind me is the class fish tank with Goldie the class pet. It was a big goldish-looking goldfish that never paid any of us kids any attention. The fish always had a look on its face, like, *"Get me out of this fish tank and set me free."* I once daydreamed that me and my UN friends snuck into the school one night and fish-napped Goldie. We took him to Central Park and put him in the pond with the other fish. The brown-skinned girl is responsible for feeding the fish this week. I was thinking the occasional look back is for Goldie, not me...umm.

Class is ending and I know that Goldie the fish needs to be fed before the bell rings. This is my chance to talk to her. The teacher gives her a pass to go feed the fish. Here we go, she will walk right past my desk. I have been prepped by my boys as to what to say. Something like, *"Hello, you look nice today."* My nerves are a wreck, I'm sweating and OMG she is up out of her chair and heading my way. She is looking right at me, and a smile comes across her face. As she passed my desk, she said hello. I opened my mouth to speak and A'...A'...That's it, close the curtain. I froze and imagined falling down a hole in the classroom floor.

My brothers and I met at the small playground after school to walk back home. I was quiet and kept to myself until Y4 asked me quietly. *"Hey, did you talk to the brown-skinned girl?"* That's all it took for Y1 & Y2 to hear. Let the sibling teasing begin! *"You are a punk! Sissy boy! That girl does not like you anyway! Punk! Punk! Punk!"* all the way home. Whew! Made it. Mom's looking out the window and hears us bickering. She gives us a look that only a mother can give her children that closes our mouths without her having to say a word. I couldn't wait until my dad came home, I needed to speak with the Man of the family.

Chapter Eleven

MUFASA

Dad worked throughout the city as a coal boiler mechanic and plumber. Most weekdays he went to work before we got up for school. It was always exciting when Dad came in from work. We would wait for him downstairs at the building entrance on the stoop and help him bring his toolbox up to the apartment. Me and Y4 were too small to handle the weight. Dad would give us his lunch box or 1 tool to carry upstairs.

He called us all his little men. He would always say I'm going to have four strong men someday. We called our dad Mufasa, it's a name that commands respect and evokes a sense of power, but also paternal love. Mufasa means king in Swahili. I always thought that my dad worked for the railroad. Every day his work attire was blue jean coveralls, boots, a light blue denim shirt, and a denim cap that looked like a conductor's hat. He always came home very dirty; Dad told us that it was the soot from the boilers he worked on. Mom always complained that she sent him out clean and he always came home dirty.

Thinking about it, she said that about us children too, dirty was our middle name. It's not like me and Y4 were trying to get dirty, but what young boy would not try to jump over a muddy puddle? And, if you made it across the first time, a second attempt is necessary, to prove that you did it. The second attempt is where I messed up and splashed dirt on my clothes.

In my mind, Dad looked like the train conductor. I read about it in a *Curious George* book. George was a little monkey that had run away from the man in the big yellow hat and was found on a train with a conductor that looked like my dad. Could my dad be hiding a little monkey somewhere and not letting us play with it? I'll ask Mom.

The apartment building was like an extended family to us, and my dad would talk to different neighbors on the way up to our apartment. He even spoke to Ms. Caribbean and her husband; she peaked around him to look at me and Y4. We had no fear at this time because we were with our dad, the King! Mr. Hawaii was waiting on the 3rd floor to speak with my dad about something, and at his feet was Major, the German Shepard. I didn't have Snoopy with me, but Major seemed a little calmer after the Snoopy incident (My Dog)!

Again, Y4 and I had no fear because we were with our dad...the King, Mufasa in the flesh. Major must have sensed that we were a little bolder than yesterday and let a low growl and put us on notice.

On the way upstairs Dad told us to leave Major alone, you boys know that that dog can eat you! Wow, Dad! Eat you?" What a message from my dad. I'm thinking that I'm gonna tell my mom what Dad said to us while he is washing up for dinner. *"Hey, mom?"* Y4 and I asked, *"Would you let Major eat us?"*

Very boldly, she said, *"Yes! You boys are getting older and won't listen to me, so, if that dog eats you, I will have less laundry and cleaning to do around here."* Y4 passes out on the floor right in front of me and starts crying, I sit on the floor with him in total shock. Whaat! Not my mom too, I'm expendable! Dad came into the kitchen and asked what was wrong, we said, *"Mom told us that Major can eat us."* Dad said, *"YUP! You boys won't do your chores and clean up your rooms and be obedient to your mom, so go wash up so that Major will have a clean meal."* *"Please, no. We will do it!"* Dad said you have fifteen minutes to get that room cleaned up. We run down the hallway screaming as we pass Y1 & Y2 on the way to our room; they ask us what's going on and we reply with *"Major is going to eat us."*

Clothes and shoes are stored properly in the closet. Old bed sheets off and clean bed sheets on with hospital corners like grandma taught us. All toys are placed in the toy box. Army men are everywhere, it's an entire battalion with tanks and artillery. Y4 and I liked our military games, but right now it was time to *bug out* and move the troops. *"Whew! Finished,"* We could hear footsteps coming down the hallway.

The door opens and Mom and Dad walk in, me and Y4 are at attention for this inspection. Our lives depended on it. Mom looks around. Dad checks under the bed and says, *"Sit down boys."* Just then, Y1 and Y2 come in carrying Y5. Mom said, *"Me and your dad love all of you very much and would never let anything happen to you, especially major eating you. We just need you to understand that following directions and doing your part is important to our family. Let me tell you a story."*

"When I was a little girl, my great, great grandmother sat me down and told me, I was good as gold." She said, *"People can become precious and as valuable as gold. You will go through the fire sometimes, and people may even kick dirt at you; not realizing that you are valuable. If you remember your teaching, guidance, and the life lesson you've learned, or even the lessons learned from the pressures of life, then you will turn out just fine and will be worth your weight in gold in this society. We love you all; You all are our "Five Gold Nuggets" and if we nurture, protect, and teach you about this life you live, someday, you also will be worth your weight in gold. Now come on and eat dinner."*

I think that was a lovely moment Mom, but; I'm still feeling some kind of way about all of this, eat your business. I was already in trouble and didn't want to mention my inner thoughts, besides, I didn't want my dad to knock my block off. I decided that obedience is better than sacrifice.

Chapter Twelve

TWO DEVILED EGGS

One day, Y4 and I were sitting in the neighborhood barbershop waiting to get a haircut. Dad sent us to the same barbershop about once a month. Afro hairstyles and shape-ups were in style, but Dad only allowed one style for his boys, which was short and tight. The barbershop was full on this day and there was a long wait to sit in a barber chair. Some of the boys were getting some good shape-ups and afro blowouts. I looked at Y4 and asked him if he wanted a shape-up. He said yes and who is going to do it? I replied, *"We can do it ourselves; I've been watching the barber for over an hour, and we can save Dad some money. Let's go."*

We went back to our apartment and got a pair of Dad's old manual hair clippers that he had in a box. I sat Y4 on a chair and put a sheet around him just like we were at the barbershop. He smiles and says, *"You know what you're doing bro." "Yes, I'm a professional and you watch the nice shape-up that you're gonna get. Next, it's my turn for you to shape me up, so pay attention."* I can barely squeeze the clippers together because they are old and stiff. *"Ouch! Be careful man and a chunk of hair falls on Y4's shoulders."* I see that I went too close, so I try to even up the other side. *Grunt. Snip. Snip. Grunt* was the sound the clippers were making every time I cut some hair. My hands are tired, so I take some Vaseline rub it all over Y4's head and say finished. I used one of Mom's mirrors like the barber does and showed him his shape up from the front. The back did not look that good and I said to myself, *It will grow back, in a day or two.*

It was my turn, and I couldn't wait to get my shape up. *"Ouch! Man, be careful!"* *"Sorry,"* Y4 said, *"I have to use both hands to cut your hair."* I see hair falling on the sheet and say this is going to look great. Dad will be happy that we saved him some money. *"Finished, Bro."* I look in the mirror, grab it, and think to myself. A little more off of the right side I take the clippers from Y4 and clip a chunk of hair off myself. That will do it. Let's clean up and get a snack.

Mom is home now, and she walks into the living room where we are watching TV and we say, *"Surprise!"* Her eyes widened and she asked, *"Who cut your hair?"* *"We did! We shaped it up ourselves to save Dad some money and he will be very surprised."* Mom said, *"Oh yes, he will be surprised."* Y1 comes into the family room next, looks at Mom, and says, *"What the Hell happened to them?"* Mom said, *"Your brothers cut their hair for their dad."* Y1 lost it and laughed loudly in his room. Mom looked at us and said, *"You two devils are in trouble, and I mean big trouble."* Now, we are a little worried that maybe we made a mistake about the haircuts, and we could still hear Y1 joined by Y2 laughing to the top of their lungs in the back room.

Dad comes home and Y4 and I can hear Mom and Dad whispering from the living room. Dad peaks in the living room and asks, *"How are my little men doing?"* and smiles at us and then rubs his head and says, *"Jesus!"* He asked us why we didn't wait at the barber shop as we were told. We sadly explained that we wanted a shapeup haircut like the other boys, and we did it ourselves to save you some money. *"Whaaaaaaaa, Whaaaaaaa, Whaaaaaaa,"* Dad said, *"Hush that crying, I will fix it, stay right here."*

Mom comes into the living room with a sheet and the old clippers we had, followed by Dad with his electric foil razor. Dad grabs Y4, sits him between his legs, and starts cutting off all his hair with the clippers. Mom does the same with me and we are both getting our heads scalped by our parents. I'm thinking why are they cutting off all the hair on our heads? Didn't they like the shape-up haircuts? We are going to look like a boiled egg. Mom said you both are like two little devils that won't listen. We will teach you both a valuable lesson today. Buzzzzzzzzz, Bzzzzzzzzzz, Dad starts shaving Y4's head with the foil razor until there is not a single hair left on top of his head. Then he calls for me, get over here you little *deviled egg*. I sit between his legs and Buzzzzzzzzzzz, Buzzzzzzzzz. All of my hair is gone. Mom rubbed some oil on both of our heads handed me a hand mirror and said, *"That's a shape-up. Now wash up and go to bed and you are both going to school tomorrow."*

I didn't sleep a wink that night; I kept thinking about how to get out of going to school the next day. I thought maybe I could fake a cold or a stomachache, but I said in my mind that Dad would only give me a spoonful of castor oil or that nasty three sixes medicine (666) that tasted worse than a cold. A hat! Yes, that's the ticket. I will wear my baseball cap all day and no one will know about my head. Y4 and I are off to school but not without Y1 & Y2 playing bongos on our heads first. Even Dad said let me rub your head for good luck. How humiliating, and to think, I still saved Dad ten dollars at the barbershop. Y4 and I head out of the building and walk to school with our friends. No one notices the bald heads because we both have baseball caps like the rest of the boys and girls. Once at school and in my classroom, I took a deep breath and thanked the Lord that I made it.

I hear the principal announce, *"Please stand and remove your hats for the Pledge of Allegiance."* I think my heart stopped beating for a few seconds as I forgot about this part of my plan. Every child in the classroom removes their hat and places their right hand across their heart, except for me. The teacher, Mr. Spoon, comes over to me, slaps my hat off my head, and says, *"You know better."*

There was a pause while the pledge was stated and then the entire classroom burst out in loud laughter and my classmates began smacking me in the head from every side. I tried to find my hat, but someone had hidden it. The teacher was also laughing and told the children to settle down, but as soon as he turned his back, *smack,* some kid hit me in the head. This went on for two straight classes until I had, had enough and a headache.

I looked and found Y4 in the guidance counselor's office because he was having the same type of day and was hiding from the kids until school ended. We both watched out of an office window as school ended for the day and all the kids were hanging around for some reason. We ran to the exit at the far side of the school and quietly slid out of the door and that's when a kid said, *"Here they are,"* and we took off running. One hundred kids must have been chasing us trying to slap us in the head. I'm thinking, *"Feet don't fail me now,"* running with one city block to go with kids yelling get those, *"Deviled Eggs."* We barely reached the apartment building when Y2 steps in the path of the boys and stops them in their tracks. All the kids knew Y2. He was big and very tall for his age. Y2 said, *"Stop chasing my brothers."* By this time, Y4 and I were all the way upstairs and in the apartment thanking God for our very lives. We both say to each other, *"No more haircuts ever."*

Chapter Thirteen

POWDER IN THE SHOE

C hurch and community service provided a strong family foundation for us. We attended church services often and participated in many community service events. Dad placed all the boys in a community military cadet group to help with discipline and guidance. This group of boys were also my close friends and we helped seniors carry their groceries to their apartments, cleaned out old vacant lots to plant community gardens, and watched out for the younger kids.

Several veterans volunteered to teach us life skills and marching drills. We learned basics and advanced marching drills and are moving to cadet rifle drills soon. Our drill team uniforms were khaki tan shirts and pants with white ascots around the neck. We wore white helmets on our heads and black combat boots on our feet. Your uniform had to be immaculate and your boots shined. One of the veterans sat us all down one day and taught us how to clean and shine our boots. The process took a long time for one shiny boot. I'm thinking, I can speed this process up with a little Vaseline. I rubbed a handful on my boots and rubbed it in with a paper towel. There, I said, the boots look just as good as Y2s who spent an hour polishing his.

Dressed in my uniform and was ready to go down the street to the bus stop where we all were going to meet. My friend said look at those dirty boots. I thought he was talking about someone else because I knew my boots were very shiny. Y3, Yes, look at your boots, and to my surprise, the boots were covered with dust. The Vaseline had become a dust and dirt magnet and collected dirt all over them for two city blocks. The drill sergeant looked down at my boots and said, *"Have them cleaned up by the drill or you're out,"* and *"You owe me 50 push-ups, 50! do you want 100? no Sir."* It took just about the entire bus ride for me to polish my boots properly.

The drill sergeant put metal taps on the heels of the boots so that a tapping sound could be heard with every maneuver. The drill team was invited to perform a drill with other community drill teams at the "Armory" near 155th Street. Our drill team is pretty good and was the fourth team in the lineup. There is also an all-girls drill team from Spanish Harlem who performed and Wowed! The crowd. They were really good and won the competition. As I was helping to pack up, I remembered noticing that during the drill Y2 had a small little cloud around him. Before I could think about it further, someone tapped me on the shoulder and said hello Y3.

I turned around and said "Wow," It was the brown-skinned girl. She looked great in her uniform. She asked, *"How are you,"* and this time I spoke up, *"I'm fine. How are you doing?"* *"I'm well also,"* she said, *"I saw you in the drills."* *"Yes, and your team did well."* Thank you, *"but your team was great and won the competition."* She thanked me and then ran back to her team on the other end of the Armory. I sighed and then noticed the boys making funny faces at me that snapped me out of it.

One day at a youth service and participating in the youth choir, the children were having a good time singing and you could feel the joy in the church. All of a sudden, near Y2, you could see this little white cloud near his feet. I tapped Y4 on his arm and said, *"Look! Y2 is on fire, or he has the Holy Spirit upon him."* Y4 smiles at me and shrugs his shoulders.

The louder we sang and the harder we clapped and patted our feet with the song, the bigger the little white cloud got. I started to imagine that it was an atomic bomb explosion plume, and I could hear the fire department in the distance. You always heard sirens from the fire department in New York City, it was a concerning coincidence. I always liked the FDNY and thought about becoming a fireman when I got older like my Uncle Ben. New York City Firemen were great people and were the only people that I knew who could walk through fire like Superman. *"Superheroes is what I called them"*

My friends and I would walk by the firehouse and see the firemen washing their trucks or setting up the water hoses. And, OMG, how we all wanted to slide down the brass *Fireman's pole.* One time the firemen let me try on a pair of boots. The boots were so big that they came up to my waist. A lady walking by stopped and said, that's the littlest fireman I've ever seen and laughed. The fireman laughed also and then said, *"Yes he is little today but will be a big strong fireman someday."* The firemen would always teach us kids about safety and how to use the corner fire call emergency box if there was a fire. I thought about pulling the corner fire alarm if I saw a fire coming from Y2.

Thank goodness the song ended; I wasn't ready to be evacuated or go to Heaven yet. I've never seen anything like that in my life. I asked Y2, *"Man, do you know you're smoking?"* He pushed me and said, *"Shut up!"* As he walked away, he was leaving white footprints behind him right out of the church's front door and to the car, forty-seven to be exact. I counted them because he pushed me. My older brothers always pushed me around and blamed me for everything. You can never be too careful when dealing with older brothers. You need a little bargaining classified information, and I could need the information as leverage in the future.

It was many weeks later, while preparing for church service when I heard Dad tell Y2, *"Don't put Y5 baby powder in your shoes anymore."* That was it, it wasn't the Holy Spirit or a ghost. It was powder put in a shoe to hopefully control Y2's stinky feet.

Chapter Fourteen

SPUD

It was almost time for spring break. The brown-skinned girl was also in my science class and sat two rows behind me. The teacher announced that we would split into teams of two students in each team for a spring break science project.

The project was to grow a plant out of a seed in a milk carton that you re-purposed from the lunchroom. The teacher called the teams and assigned each of us a seed. I had no idea that I was sitting in an odd seat. She said, "Y3." I answered, "Yes." She said, *"I will come back to you, but you have a potato."* She continued down the roll until she told the brown-skinned girl, you are with Y3." I could feel her eyes on the back of my head as I slowly turned around to see her smile at me. Fireworks! Nervous twitch in my leg, I can't breathe. Can't breathe.

I had a conversation with my mom about her. Mom smiled and said, *"My nice boy, pretend you're talking to me and breathe. You will be fine."* I remember Mom's words, so the next time, I will be able to say hello. The teacher asked us to line up with our partners and prepare our seeds for germination. We put soil in the milk carton with a measured quarter cup of water. The potato was small enough to fit in the carton and we named it *SPUD*. Now, SPUD was a tan-colored smooth young potato, from a proud Idaho family. All the science projects were lined up on a large black window seal ledge and in front of the window ledge there was a large metal radiator that kept the classroom warm.

Even though it was early spring it was still very cool in the mornings. Because all the milk cartons looked the same, she wrote SPUD on ours to differentiate our project from everyone else's. I noticed leaving the classroom that SPUD was pushed closer to the window ledge's edge. Oh well, I said, inside my head, he will be fine. All the students packed their belongings and headed for the hallway to line up for dismissal. Five days with no school, I can stay up late and play with my friends all day. The week went by quickly and then it was time to go back to school.

I saw the brown-skinned girl in line for science class and asked her how her spring break was. Her family went on a trip, and she was excited to see if SPUD had grown any. Science was the first class of the day, and the teacher was running late. The classroom lights were still off, and solar system posters covered the window so you couldn't see in. Here comes the teacher. She apologized for being late. She unlocked the door and turned on the lights. To our surprise, there was SPUD!

"No," the brown-skinned girl said, *"He's gone!"* All I could see was the empty carton with dirt spilling out. As I got closer, poor SPUD was lying on top of the radiator vent. Dried and air-fried for a whole week. What a shock to the class, you would have thought we lost our best friend. Even though some other science projects were sprouting green leaves. Everyone was focused on SPUD. Kids sniffing, someone saying, *"Why, Spud, Why?"* The teacher asked everyone to take their seats and calm down.

Just then, you heard the brown-skinned girl's soft voice say, *"Spud, when I grow up, I'm gonna mash you up, with butter on your side."* She then said it repeatedly until the entire class sang, *"WHEN I GROW UP, I'M GONNA MASH YOU UP WITH BUTTER ON YOUR SIDE."*

After class, she and I picked SPUD up. He looked like an old crispy potato wedge someone left in a fryer. We put him back in the milk carton and the teacher said she would take care of the rest.

Chapter Fifteen

BUTTER BEAN

I t was difficult for Dad and Mom at times to raise five children in a large city. Dad worked all the time to keep a roof over our heads. He would complain about the food prices all the time and tell us that we were eating him out of house and home. We all would go with our parents to the grocery store and help bag the food. Mom would teach us how to shop and how to spot the best sales. She kept a grocery list in her purse and would call out the food items for us to place in the cart. Things like bread, potatoes, grits, cereal, and *"Butter Beans."*

I was always a picky eater and had to adjust my taste buds to meet Mom's cooking style. Mom was the best creative chef I knew and could make leftovers taste like steak. The assembly lines of breakfast, lunch, and dinner seemed to never stop, and Mom could be found many days reviewing homework lessons in the kitchen with flour on her face from baking. With so many children Dad and

Mom placed some type of bean on the menu at least three times a week. Pinto beans, kidney beans, and *butter beans*. I despised *butter beans,* Mom said they were good for you.

The first thing I noticed is that there is no butter in these beans. Mom would simmer them in a white gravy or sauce and serve them over white rice ewe! nasty! Some adults told a big fat lie to us kids that these beans were good for you. Grandma called them *Lima Beans* and they were green simmered in green sauce, and again…ewe! nasty. At least three times a week I got popped by my parents for eating the rice out of the bowl and leaving the beans. Mom finally gave up and told me *"Butter Beans Just don't agree with me."*

Everyone has memories of a childhood friend, that they liked or disliked. This kid was a strong dislike! All my family knew that me and *Butter Bean* did not get along. He was a big bully and a snitch, and as my uncle would say, *"Snitches get stitches."*

He was a big fat kid, outweighed me by 100 pounds, and was taller than most of the kids in the fourth grade. He was an Italian boy, and his family owned the neighborhood delicatessen. Me and my brothers always said that he probably ate up all the bologna and cheese and that's what made him fat. We were both the same age, but because of his size, he looked much older than me. He constantly picked on the smaller children and if I saw it, I would intervene. I was small for my age but a fearless street fighter like Batman. Unfortunately, being a small guy in Harlem NY, you had to fight to survive. My dad and Uncles taught me exceptionally good urban city survival skills.

A few weeks after the Forbidden Alley incident, I was at the park and noticed Butter Bean talking to *my* brown-skinned girl. After poor SPUD passed away I and the brown-skinned girl had become friends and I would walk her to the school bus. On some days, we would play at the park. Now, Butter Bean was trying to move in on "my girl" (unofficially, not my girlfriend yet), but I was working on it. At this point, I realize Butter Bean is trying to get my attention. This fight has been brewing for several weeks now.

I talked with my dad about this bully. He advised me to speak up for myself and tell that boy to leave me alone or he's gonna have a fight on his hands. My Uncle advised me to pick up a brick and "knock the hell out of him," but I followed my dad's advice. Butter Bean sees me walking towards the playground, hits the brown-skinned girl in the arm, and runs towards the softball field. I ran to the brown-skinned girl and asked if she was all right. She said, *"Yes,"* and then said something loud in Spanish.

Suddenly, three big boys show up and she points to Butter Bean who is still running towards the softball field while holding her arm. They looked at me with wondering looks, and she said, *"He is my boyfriend."* My mind starts to drift and see the fireworks in the sky and my heart is doing something weird also. She says, *"My brothers will get him."* *"You have brothers,"* I asked her. *"Yes, three older brothers and one sister."* I didn't know she had brothers and big brothers at that.

My Mom once told me that Jesus would fight my battles for me. Well today, *J E S U S* came in the form of *Carlos, Fernando, and Julio.* These boys took off in a full sprint towards Butter Bean; who when he saw them coming began to run in a zig-zag pattern. His out-of-shape little chubby legs began to give out and he fell to the grass panting for air. That did not stop the three brothers from whomping on him for a few minutes.

Meanwhile, I bought myself and my girlfriend coconut shaved ice for refreshment. To my surprise, off in the distance, I could see three tall figures and one short figure that was limping coming towards us. She said, *"Look, my brothers are returning."* *"Wow!"* I said they had Butter Bean's hands behind his back, and he was crying. They walked right up to us. And one of the brothers slapped him on the back of the head and he said, *"I'm sorry!"* *"Louder!"* *"I'm Sorry!"* I will never touch you or him nor speak or look at you again."

Chapter Sixteen

I HAVE A GIRL FRIEND

"**H**ey *Mom, guess what happened to me today?*" Mom was busy doing the princess's hair, again. How many hairstyles does she need? This is an everyday appointment with Mom and is encroaching on my face-to-face mom time. "Mom, mom, mom, mom,"...All right boy! Even the princess seemed annoyed, like she was the priority in the family now, with that look, as if to say, *"Move on peasant boy. Say what you have to say. You have ten seconds."* She was also acting busy doing her doll's hair by mimicking Mom. I calmed down and said, The brown-skinned girl said, *"I am her boyfriend."* It took all my energy to get the words out. Mom calmly responded, *"That's nice; now go wash your hands and help your dad with dinner."*

I was crushed by the lack of enthusiasm about my girlfriend's good news, and it was all the princess's fault. I walked into the kitchen with my head down and my dad was preparing dinner. He was a surprisingly good cook, and several times a week he would prepare breakfast or dinner. Dad looked at me and asked, *"What's the matter man?"* *"Well, Dad, I have a girlfriend."* "The brown-skinned girl" Dad turned around and said, *"That's my little man."* *"She is very pretty,"* and *"I know her Father and family."*

This was my first girlfriend, and I had no clue what I was supposed to do. Dad took a break from cooking and said, *"Let me explain something to you son."* I'm thinking here we go! I'm a big boy now and it's time for the birds and the bees to talk. I sat quietly in the chair next to him and he explained that I must always be polite and respectful to girls and boys at all times, and to treat people like I want to be treated. I'm thinking, *that's it.* I said to myself, *Dad knows best.* I took the advice to boost my little man's ego.

Dad went back to cooking and I then heard Y4 whisper, *"You got a girlfriend,"* *"You got a girlfriend."* *"Be quiet, before I get you back."* He decides to hum it, "hum, hum, hum, hum. hum"… Dad!" *"You boys cut it out and set the table for dinner."* Punch, *"Ow! He hit me."* *"So sorry, it was an accident."* Dad gave me a look that said, *I will not tolerate you boys fighting each other; you both know the house rules.*

The princess was also getting older and seemed to take it all in stride, she didn't seem to care about the bickering coming from her brothers. She watched her brothers' mistakes and avoided them, so she rarely gets punished for anything, she gets new clothes all the time while I have to wear Y1 stinky hand-me-downs, and she has her own chauffeur and security detail. Y5 just plays with her dolls and doll houses all the time. She recently went to a Broadway show and upon returning home announced that she is now to be addressed as "Queen Ester." Mom thought it was cute, Y1 said, *"Who the hell is Queen Ester,"* I said Y5. I just kept quiet, and I wasn't trying to get in any more trouble with my smart mouth. I smirk, and think to myself, If Y5 wants to be called "Queen Ester," oh well then.

One day I accidentally left about one hundred or so army men in her room. *Accidentally.* She stepped on an army man and hurt her little foot. That alerted the Y2 security agent and got me in trouble again. You would have thought I stole her doll house. She put on a drama show for Y1 and Y2 that could have won an Oscar. Y1 called me selfish and ordered me to clean it up immediately. He said, *"I am in charge of you and will let Mom know your punishment. My punishment was sustained by the higher court of my mom, and it was to clean up all the army men including cleaning the princess's room. So sorry, I meant "Queen Ester."* I thought that this was unfair judiciary practices, and I'm calling my lawyer.

Most of the time I didn't venture into the princess's area. She had her own room, closet, laundry basket, and many dolls. Some of the dolls talked and cried and they all had beedi little eyes. She had as many dolls as I had army men. Dad had built shelves over her dresser that went to the ceiling. All types of dolls were on the shelves and seemed to watch you or accidentally fall off the shelf and scare the "bejesus" out of you. There was one large "Raggedy Ann" doll hanging off the shelf and looked like it was gonna fall down any minute. I saw it hanging there but said it's not mine so if it falls, it falls.

Huffing and puffing, I began cleaning up the army men in Y5s, "dang it," "Queen Ester's" room. This was a big room, and she had more floor space than any of her brother's "peasant rooms." However, It was perfect for military game night operations. Y4 and I reviewed the plans carefully and had the secret *go codes* for tonight. The goal was to search and destroy the enemy doll house and capture "Barbie. That's when Y5, "Dang it" I'm not gonna keep writing "Queen Ester." "It's my book and she is Y5."

All the army men were picked up and I began to clean up the room when suddenly the lights went out. The lights would go off in our building and neighborhood sometimes. I froze as my eyes adjusted to the darkness, I thought, what's going on? and I look around to see many sets of eyes looking back at me. Just then, the large "Raggedy Ann" doll fell off the top shelf and scared me. I started moving backward toward the door and accidentally tripped on a blanket and closed it. I then fell on a "Chatty Cathy" doll that talked and said, *"Take me with you."* Right then, I jumped up and said help!

As I tried to kick the blanket and doll, from in front of the door. The doll said again "Take me with you," and the "Raggedy Ann" doll seemed to be sitting up or trying to stand up. I'm thinking, "El No," as I tried to open the door, it would not open, "Help," I cried out again. I didn't realize Y1 was holding the doorknob from the other side preventing me from opening it until I heard him say. "You're grown now." Stay in there in the "Valley of the Dolls." I continue to pull on the doorknob until I finally get out of the room. Y1 ran into the darkness before I could get my hands on him. I'm

mad, scared, and thinking " Y1 will be eaten by Major someday,"
"I will make sure of it."

Chapter Seventeen

THE FIGHT

Mom had a saying, *"You go, we all go."* She taught us to stick together and never fight our brothers or sisters. But if someone challenges or attacks you, then they attack us all. One day while playing stoop ball across the street from our building in an open basement or "pit" as we kids called it. It is where all the kids played sometimes and was an alternative play area other than the street. Our street was always full of kids because we had a small basketball court behind the church near the center of the city block. It was closer for kids to play "B-ball" at the church than to walk the two blocks to the community center.

On this day the block seemed to be loaded with kids, jumping rope, skateboarding, throwing the football, and riding bikes. *Stoop ball* was an inner-city game where you bounced a tennis ball off the edge of a stoop step. If the ball was caught, then it was out and if the ball got past the catcher, then you scored a point.

Y1 and Y2 were playing stoop ball and had won several games and some of the other big boys got mad. The big boys started pushing Y1 and that's when suddenly, a fight broke out between them with boys from another neighborhood. This was quickly becoming a wrestling mania event as other boys started jumping in the pit to fight. And that included me and Y4, some big kid kicked me in the neck, and I fell against the corner wall holding it. Then all of a sudden, some big kid stood over me and began throwing other kids to the left and right like a little ninja. I looked up and to my surprise, it was Butter Bean. He was picking big kids up and body-slamming them on top of one another. Kids began running and jumping out of the pit to get away from the fight. Y2 picks me up and asks if I am all right. I say, *"I want the boy who kicked me."* By that time, the fight is over, and the boys are clearing out of the pit because parents were alerted of the fight and the parental warnings were being shouted to stop fighting and come home now!

We climbed out of the pit standing together as brothers looking side to side at each other a little bruised and scratched, but together. While walking across the street to our building, I heard someone call out to me saying, *"I got him, the one who kicked you."* I turned around to see Butter Bean holding up his fist! I got him for you. Interesting...I'm still too young to understand the "Make your enemies your footstool," or "turn-the-other-cheek theory." I wanted to personally punch the kid who kicked me.

The days seemed to be getting shorter, and darker, and even the clouds looked meaner. Everyone seemed to be fighting during this time. My uncle called it the "Dark Days of Harlem."

Chapter Eighteen

THE DARK DAYS

Things were changing in Harlem. *Blue Magic* had hit the streets and taken it by storm. Drugs and alcoholism were consuming many people in my community. Neighborhood people were getting mugged and robbed of their belongings daily. Mom, Dad, or another adult had to escort us to and from school and events due to the number of drug addicts hanging around the street corners. My Uncle Blue and Uncle White were NYC police officers at the 28th Precinct in Harlem. The precinct was near West 123rd St. and on 8th Avenue, and these brave men and women helped watch over us and the community.

We only traveled in groups of five or more to part the Red Sea as we called it. Sometimes, there were so many drug addicts the sidewalk would be full, so when they saw you coming, they would break apart, and you would have a path to walk through. There were fires and the police sirens were always blaring through the neighborhood. Terrible, violent fights would break out on the street at any time. It did not matter if kids were playing or not, you just ran for cover and tried to get to the apartment building. Heroin, methadone, and cocaine were plentiful all across Harlem and were taking their toll on the community.

I remember President Johnson speaking on the radio about the drug epidemic in the United States. Mayor Wagner was also challenged with how to control the drug problem in New York City. My Mom and Dad kept us very close, and our playground was more in the house than on the neighborhood streets. One day, Y2 and I were walking down our street when two men approached us and asked us to do them a favor. They said they would give us ten dollars each if we carried a package to 125th Street. Now, ten dollars was a lot of money back then for a kid. But Y2 remembered what Uncle Blue told us about carrying packages for strangers and saying no to drugs. *"No,"* was his answer and we walked away; of course, I was thinking how much candy I could have bought for ten bucks. Let me say, *"Big Brother's actions were correct."* We were always taught not to speak or take anything from a stranger. And besides that, I did not want to be eaten by Major, The thought, still bothers me.

The building we lived in was falling apart, sometimes the heat didn't work, and it would be very cold. We had a gas fireplace that kept the apartment warm on most days. For some reason, there was a shortage of light bulbs in Harlem. Because we only had three working in our building's hallway. I was always scared coming into the building and walking up the dark staircase by myself. And of course? Whose door was open on the second floor with that light shining in the hallway. The Caribbean family and Ms. Caribbean calmly said, *"Y3, don't be scared of me. I will walk you upstairs to your apartment because the lights are off up there."*

She shined a flashlight up the steps, and I began to walk in front of her. I pretended to fall on a step, so I could see if she was walking or floating. "Kiss a brick," is what my uncle would say, I couldn't see a thing and her feet did not step on my hands. I am quickly thinking of how to escape and not be placed in a pot for dinner. She said, *"See, we are almost there,"* and my Mom opened the door, and I ran past her while saying thank you to Ms. Caribbean. All night long I dreamt that I was being stewed in a pot with carrots and onions.

Chapter Nineteen

DR. KING

Thursday, April 4, 1968, it's a cool damp spring evening, but something is wrong! Too quiet for the chain gang. I hear the family gathering in the family room. We had a black and white TV there and I could hear, *"This is a CBS special Report from Walter Cronkite announcing, "Dr. King has died!"* Dr. King was standing on the balcony of a second-floor hotel room tonight when a shot was fired from across the street. In the friend's words, the bullet exploded in his face when Dr. Martin Luther King, Jr. was assassinated in Memphis.

"Dr. Martin Luther King, the apostle of non-violence in the Civil Rights Movement, has been shot to death in Memphis, Tennessee. Police have issued an all-points bulletin for a well-dressed, young white man seen running from the scene. Officers also reportedly chased and fired on a radio-equipped car containing two white men."

My dad and uncles were upset. Saying things like *"I can't believe this. They killed our brother the preacher."* *"Sons of Mitches"* followed by "Right is right," and "Wrong is wrong." People started gathering in the street crying and yelling, "We shall overcome! We won't go quietly. We are somebody!" I am very scared at this point. Police and fire trucks with sirens sounding are up and down the avenue. You can smell the smoke in the air. Then Bang, Bang, Bang. Gunshots. Mom brings all of us to the center hallway and tells us to sit on the floor, we will be fine.

There is a heavy knock on the door. Who is it? Blue and again Blue & white. Blue & white were my uncles, both NYC police officers. *"Are you all ok? Where are the children?"* We were huddled together in the center of the hallway surrounded by Mom, Dad, our uncle, and aunts. My uncles said, *"We had to get that crazy Hawaii man and dog out of the way."* He wouldn't let us pass.

The UN was on lockdown, and Mr. Hawaii had barricaded the entrance door with Major at his side. Uncle White said It was crazy outside and people were very upset over the assassination of Dr. Martin Luther King Jr. Blue said we are staying here until the National Guard arrives to restore order in the streets. This was the scariest time of my life. I thought we were all gonna die. The smell of smoke, sirens, gunshots, noise, screaming, and yelling lasted all night long into the early morning. *"Wake up!"* Mom said, *"We have to go."* Dad, Uncle Blue, and Uncle White escorted all of us downstairs to the car, a tan station wagon. I looked around and began to cry, our neighborhood looked like a bomb had gone off. Buildings and cars were burning, and I saw a man lying in the street.

Dad pushed my head down and told me to keep it down. My dad was driving fast, and our bodies were moving from side to side with each turn. They took us to Grandma's house in the Bronx for a few days.

The news of Dr. King's assassination was felt in this community also; however, it was quieter in the Bronx. Grandma hustled us into the building and upstairs to her apartment on the third floor. My Uncles secured the path to the apartment and then headed back to the police station. We all were safe now; Grandma's house was always a safe space. I walked into Grandma's bedroom to check on her. You could tell she was sad as she sat in her favorite chair by the window. She said you know Y3, trouble knocks on everyone's door sometimes. The only way to get past life's troubles is to pray and stay positive because *"Trouble doesn't last always."*

Chapter Twenty

GRANDMA'S HOUSE

G randma was my buddy; she was a short Cuban woman from the South with the same caramel-colored skin as my Mom. She had long black and silver, grey hair and was always dressed very nicely. She loved her grandchildren and visited us several times a week. She lives in a small apartment in a large brown building in the southern section of the Bronx. This section of the Bronx was occupied by Latinas, Puerto Ricans, Dominicans, and Cubans.

The mixture of diverse cultures in this community was wonderful. When you entered grandma's apartment building you could smell the aroma of varied spices coming from the different apartments. Grandma always talked to and was visited by her friends. One of her best friend was a Spanish woman who was a doctor in pediatric medicine. She was very nice to me, and I called her my auntie. She always taught me lessons about first aid and would let me use her stethoscope to hear my heartbeat.

I would go with her to the neighborhood clinic and help out. I mostly cleaned up or stocked supplies. She told me that she would like for me to come visit her in Puerto Rico so she could fatten me up and begin my training to become a doctor someday. Grandma thought it was a good idea and said she always wanted a doctor in the family. This fattening-me-up idea was always on my grandma's mind for me. She pushed three meals a day on me plus snacks every time I visited her. Biscuits, eggs, bacon, grits, oatmeal, and cereal were just part of the menu. No Ma'am, I'm not hungry did not work for me at grandma's house. When I left to go back home I felt like a stuffed turkey.

Across the street from the building was a small park with a playground for kids. We played on the chain-linked swings and a wooded seesaw and basketball court. My friend Carlos and I would play in the park most of the day. One of our favorite games was *Lottie's*. It was similar to marbles, but all you needed was a soda pop cap and some gum. We did not have money for a bag of marbles. You drew a circle on the sidewalk and chewed gum; chewed until all the sugar was gone. Then packed it in the bottle cap to give it a little weight. This made the bottle cap slide across the sidewalk with just a little pluck of your finger. The goal was to knock your opponent's bottle cap out of the circle.

Someone called out "Charlie Brown!" Snoopy was with me and started barking first because he heard her voice. This was how your family got your attention in the Bronx and if you didn't respond someone would tell you that your mom or dad was calling you. I ran to a spot under my grandma's window, *"Yes Ma'am. Are you all, right?"* *"Yes, Ma'am. OK, one more hour, and then come into the house for dinner."* *"Yes, Ma'am!"* While running back to the Lottie's game, I heard something. Conga said, *"Carlos, the band is getting together for a tribute to Dr. King. That is a steel Caribbean drum you hear here now. My uncle plays it."* 'Let's go check it out,' music can soothe the soul. A lady was singing the song, "We Shall Overcome," with Latin Caribbean soul music accompanying her. People began to gather and hold hands while the music played. You could feel that Dr. Martin Luther King, Jr. was there with you. What a day!

Chapter Twenty-One

ANGRY BIRDS

We are back in Harlem now; the neighborhood is clean, and things are quiet. Even the sidewalks are clear because the drug addicts moved to another location. Things were getting back to normal and some of the kids started playing outside again. I often asked my Mom why we did not hang our washed clothes out over the alleyway like our neighbors. Mom explained that those damn pigeons would poop all over her clean laundry every time and that made her so mad.

She also mentioned the flying underwear incident, which embarrassed her. One of our chores was to fold and put away our laundry once Mom washed it. One day, while folding laundry in the living room with the window open, we all start having a clothes fight, throwing clean clothes at each other, and having fun when suddenly the wind grabs a pair of my Dad's underwear midair and begins to rotate them like a flying saucer out of the window. We run to the window and watch the underwear land right on top of a man's head. OMG! The man saw us duck back in the window and yelled a curse word. We knew we were in big trouble when Mom came in holding the underwear in her hand. Let us just say that the chastisement hurt.

I did not know what was worse than the rats of New York City until I tangled with the New York City pigeon gang. The pigeons seemed to work in unison against us kids. One day, while playing stickball in the street, my friend accidentally hit a pigeon and it fell to the ground. We gathered around it feeling remorse and trying to figure out what to do next.

All of a sudden, about fifty pigeons, or the "117th Street Pigeon Gang," as they are now known came from everywhere and began to dive bomb on the kids and adults in the street. I remembered an old war-flying ace movie where the pilot was dropping bombs on a target. It sounded like, "Click"… "click"…" Bombardier to pilot. Open the bomb doors." You could almost hear the "whistle!" "Rat-Ta-Ta-Ta!" "Splat! Splat! Splat." Pigeon poop was flying everywhere, and kids and adults were running for cover. Some kid said, "Save yourself!" "Save yourself!" "Mama!"

Cars stopped as they too were bombarded with dive-bombing pigeons and poop. One man tried to hit one with an umbrella trying to fight them off and was quickly targeted by the pigeons for an all-out air assault. This lasted every bit of ten minutes according to the clock in the window of the dry cleaners across the street. These dam pigeons were determined to fly, fight, and win. Maybe they were covert pigeons for the United States *Pigeon* Force. These pigeons were well organized and flew like a squadron. They finally met their match when they bombed a green and white police car, the police officers sounded the car siren. The siren's piercing sound must have scared them into flight, and they left the area. People began coming out of their shelters and sounding; the coast was clear. Someone said, *"Damn those pigeons. Damn those pigeons to hell."*

Chapter Twenty - Two

THE RATS

In 1972, Michael Jackson released a song named *Ben*. There was also a movie released in 1971 titled "Willard." Ben was a rat and his family lived in New York City and a few of his cousins lived in my building's old dumbwaiter system. The movie "Ratatouille" could not compare to our building rats.

It was no secret that New York City had a major rodent problem in the 1960s and 1970s. You could see rats throughout the city. Sanitation and trash piles on the city streets were part of the problem. I will never forget the morning newspaper that said, *"Rat Attack Near City Hall."* The number one nightmare scenario of every New Yorker: is coming into close physical contact with *"Rattus Norvegious,"* or the typical city street and sewer rat. Now imagine being attacked by a horde of these greasy creatures. That's what happened to one woman while heading to her car parked on a street near city hall.

The rats were having a field day and night. In our kitchen was an old, abandoned dumbwaiter. It was used in the late 1940s to deliver packages to each apartment building floor. It had been abandoned and seemed to be a meeting place for the rats. My Dad would hear the rats in the dumbwaiter climbing the old ropes. Dad would slowly open the old dumbwaiter door, hit the rope with a baseball bat, and then close the door. You would hear, thump, thump, thump. Rats hitting the bottom of the dumbwaiter.

This was a strange form of entertainment to me; I did not like rats and I'm sure they didn't like me. As a young man, it was also strange to me that I knew the difference between rats. Harlem had grey rats, while the Bronx had black rats, and the Lower East Side had possums. We called the possums (Boss Rats). We would help Dad cover holes in the apartment with the tin metal he had. The rats would try to scratch through the wall in the kitchen near the dumbwaiter. We were always on guard in case one got into the apartment. A large rat trap was waiting for it; it was an unpleasant sight to see a rat caught in a trap. Guts and blood all over the place that had to be cleaned up.

One day while playing field hockey in that alley behind the building. Not to be confused with the forbidden alley. A rat jumps right in the playing field. You would have thought that we kids were playing for the NHL. I could hear the announcer in my head say, "Smack!" "The rat is hit with the hockey stick," and pushed to #17. "#17 lines up for the goal shot but is blocked by #6." "#6 is checked by #2," and, "smack the rat flies into the wall." "#4 checks #6 and lines up for a goal shot." "GOAL!" We played hockey with that rat until it stopped moving. Oh well, game over! What a life for a city kid in Harlem.

Chapter Twenty-Three

LIGHTS OUT

The Y5 are getting older and times are changing. These teenage years bring lots of changes to our minds and bodies. We have always experienced brownouts or blackouts in New York City but today It's dark everywhere and I'm making my way down the apartment hallway by feeling the walls until I get to the family room. "Hello," Mom said I'm here by the window, what's going on? It's a city-wide blackout. No one has any power at their homes and all the city streetlights are out. Mom was listening to one of Dad's small transistor radios he uses to listen to baseball games. The radio announcer said, "Stay in your homes for safety. This is the New York City Emergency Broadcast System." "City Wide Black Out." All of us were in the family room together and boy was it hot! The apartment didn't have an air conditioner and we would use several electric fans to circulate cool air around the apartment. Due to the power outage, the apartment had no fresh air movement. We all were using pieces of cardboard to fan each other trying to keep cool.

Looking out the window, all you could see were car headlights and dark figures running. Fire trucks and police cars with sirens blaring were driving up and down the avenue. Bang! Bang! Y1 said, that sounds like gunshots, Mom ordered us away from the windows. A loud crash could be heard with yelling and screaming and sirens nearby. Knock, knock, knock followed by knock, knock, knock was the family code. Mom said wait here let me go see who is at the door. "Wait here. I don't think so," when mom moved out of the family room, so did the Y5 who stood right behind her. She said where are all of you going and Y1 said, "You go, we all go." Who is it? "Bro," he was my mom's brother who then said *open the door*. Mom had a candle in her hand and could see her brother's face as she let him in. "I need some help. What kind of help do you need Bro?" Let me show you, the stairwell landing was full of all kinds of things, clothes, food, and furniture. Where did you get this stuff from? People are looting all the stores in the area and this stuff was given to me. Mom replied, "Given or stolen? You are a fool" You are destroying our community. I don't want any of this stuff, take it away. But sis, "But sis what" and she closed the door.

We all slept together in the family room that night, everyone was too scared to go to their own room. The noise went on all night long and it didn't quite down until finally, the sun began to peek through the clouds. Daybreak was here, Y4 and I peeked out the window, and what a sight to see. Our neighborhood was destroyed, people's cars were burning, the dry cleaners were on fire and the corner grocery store looked like a bomb had gone off in it. The ice boxes were sitting on the sidewalk empty and turned over. Window and car glass were all over the street and sidewalk. An ambulance medic was attending to a wounded lady across the street. Mom was awakened by our talk and came over to the window to take a look. She crossed her arms and said, "What a mess we have made." "We didn't do it, Mom." "I know it, not my *gold nuggets*." By saying "US" I mean the people living right in this community.

We sat in a circle near her and listened, *"Fools, Fools, Fools' ' People know better, but still exhibit this bad behavior, they think it is all right to take what doesn't belong to them. It looks shiny and you want it badly, so you take it, clearly knowing that it doesn't belong to you but, you are blinded by the shininess and find out that it wasn't what you thought it was. It's "Fools Gold" "Everything that's shiny isn't gold and everything that glimmers is not a diamond. When people are looking for fool's gold, they "Take anything that doesn't belong to them," "They lie" "They cheat, Scam, and are Self-destructive. "everyone has the power to change" and if someone tells you "They can't change or they were born like this" Then you tell them to be "Born Again", and "Jesus Loves You". "Do you hear me Children" "Yes Mom". My children were made from real gold and If your children want to find the real gold in you, just look in the mirror, and if you don't see what you want to see "Clean the Mirror."*

We watched the business owners and property owners clean up from the looting. Some were very upset and openly asked why would you do this? Why would you let a bunch of fools destroy your neighborhood? People also helped with the cleanup and even washed some of the blood off of the streets and sidewalks. It was late in the afternoon before the power in Harlem was restored and there were several days of brownouts before the power normalized. The grocery store and the cleaners didn't recover and closed permanently in our neighborhood because the owners lost all they had because of the looting and fires.

Chapter Twenty-Four

FOOLS GOLD

I t's a cosmic process to create "Real Gold" and may take many
years for just the right moment, it might take thousands of
years until it's just the right time. Some people lack patience
and rush the gold-making process only to discover that they have
wound up with "Fool's Gold."

"Fools Goal" is a popular nickname for a mineral called
"Pyrite." The mineral earned itself the name because it's yellow and
shiny and to put it simply, boasts incredible resemblance to gold.
"Fool's Gold" and "Real Gold" are two worlds apart; "Gold is a
metal and has value" and "Fools Gold is an iron sulfide mineral and
has little value." An ounce of Pyrite is worth twenty-one dollars
whereas an ounce of Gold is worth over one thousand dollars.

Pyrite is an often-overlooked material today although it has
been instrumental in enabling many aspects of our modern culture

and industry. This bright, brassy mineral is the most abundant metal sulfide in the Earth's crust. Most people today are familiar with the mineral, even though they do not know its details because it stands out in the natural environment and because of the connection with "Fool's Gold." Pyrite has been a source of both metals and sulfur since ancient times.

In my Harlemite community today, things have changed over the years. People have become more depressed and hardened by the racial and economic pressures of the big city's daily life. Positivity is far and few in between because of the dark day's and many of the communities' "Gold Nuggets" have chosen to hide themselves for fear of becoming consumed by "Fool's Gold." My grandmother once asked me a question in anger due to my "Fool-ager" actions. She said, "A real golden person has value, and a fool doesn't. **Which One Are You?"**

Chapter Twenty-Five

EXPERIENCES

I'm older now, and I wouldn't change growing up in Harlem, New York for anything in the world. Yes, the struggle and dark days were very real. The good far outweighed the bad. There were marvelous times and experiences, like the African American parade that marched down Seventh Avenue each fall around September. The HBCU marching bands like Grambling University, Howard University, and Morgan State University to name a few would high-step through Harlem encouraging the young people to go to college. You could find a Harlem Historian and Harlemites around every corner willing to tell you about their story. You could also visit many of the historic sites like the "Hotel Theresa," which was once called the Waldorf of Harlem opened in the year 1913 on 125th Street and 7th Avenue.

Back then it was an all-white clientele and staff apartment building, thirteen stories high with three hundred rooms. In 1940, the hotel began accepting all races and hired black staff and management. Many black performers and politicians gave speeches and performed in Manhattan but were not accepted in mid-Manhattan hotels. The Hotel Theresa accepted these great people and treated them respectfully. We would visit the Apollo Theater and see performances from famous rock and roll, gospel, and jazz artists, like Aretha Franklin, Tina Turner, Smoky Robinson, BB King, James Brown, and Gladys Knight. There was always lots to see and experience like the Museum of Natural History and the Metropolitan Museum of Art " the Met" found in mid-Manhattan. We would also travel by subway train to Battery Park and catch the ferry to the Statue of Liberty on Ellis Island.

Harlem provided great cultural experiences, teaching, and nurturing me with life lessons, guidance, and understanding from some great teachers and historians. I struggled with some life lessons because I forgot my teachings and fell for "Fool's Gold" at times. With continued support and help, those hard lessons provided just enough of a collision to make me a "gold nugget of today."

ABOUT THE AUTHOR

H e mentors young men and serves in his community. His passion for writing stretches back many generations to his grandparents who wrote poems and maps for family and the community. His goal of this book is to simply tell his story. Born and raised in Harlem New York.  Charles (Chuck) Dixon is a family man who trusts God and enjoys the great outdoors. He is an avid sports fan and enjoys fishing, music, traveling and politics.

Contact author at: 5goldnuggets1@gmail.com